An In-depth Case Study on Nonprofit Organization's Resource Allocation and Operational Optimization

SECOND EDITION 2

Second Chance

Noriko I. Chapman
with Dr. Daryl D. Green

About the Cover:

Photography:
Mt. Fuji by Takaaki Kumazawa
Noriko Chapman by DIGI-QUEST Photography

Cover Design: David Williams

Second Chance:

An In-depth Case Study on Nonprofit Organization's Resource Allocation and Operational Optimization

Noriko I. Chapman
with Dr. Daryl D. Green

Second Edition

"How Noriko generated such positive recognition for our Center has been amazing. Her insight and willingness to advocate for our needs in the community have improved our Center operations, which has directly impacted the lives of our clients in such a positive way. Her journey to our doorstep is one of strength, persistence, faith and a willing heart to share her business knowledge with others. Her story is one that needs to be shared with others. "

Deborah C. Quillen

Tennessee Rehabilitation Center Manager

VR Field Supervisor 1

"Noriko Chapman has used her personal challenges and professional expertise to help others improve their working environment, their lives and their community. Through hard work, dedication and compassion she explains how small changes can make a big difference in the nonprofit environment. Her belief in herself and her faith in others shine through."

Debra J. Sullivan, Ph.D.

Program Director

The Cancer Support Community – East TN

"Noriko Chapman has provided a great insight into the responsibility and contribution that we all can make in our community. The benefits will reach well into the future helping to influence a more diverse society."

Don Tracy

Director, Denso Manufacturing TN, Inc.

"As Director of the Lincoln Memorial University MBA program, I believe we need to challenge our students to reach levels of understanding and achievement they initially thought impossible. While this is a worthy goal, it is critical that our students apply their new knowledge and experience to the real world. Only through this can we impact the lives of others. With the help of others who applied their knowledge, Noriko overcame what initially seemed impossible. Noriko was able to resume her studies at LMU, and through Dr. Green's class and encouragement, Noriko is applying her understanding, knowledge and experience to assist and dramatically impact the lives of others. "

Michael E. Dillon, Jr., Ph.D

Director, MBA Program

Department Chair Assistant Professor of Business

Lincoln Memorial University School of Business

"Noriko Chapman writes a moving story about how her encounter with cancer brings blessings to the Tennessee Vocational Rehabilitation Center, her company, and her family. As an MBA student, she used her expertise about organizational change to implement a program that provided work for handicapped workers at a quality necessary for auto parts. In the process she went through the steps of planning changing, training workers, creating production schedules and implementing the new program. Her story demonstrates both her business competence and her love for others."

Scott Brunger, Ph.D

Professor of Economics, Maryville College

Special appreciation to Robert & Heather Williams for taking the

photographs of

Noriko Chapman

For more information or suggestions, please contact:

Ms. Noriko Chapman

PMLA

P.O. Box 32733

Knoxville, TN 37930

Phone: (865) 379-6455

Email: Chance2.Noriko@gmail.com

<u>Dedication</u>

We dedicate this book to all who do not give up and continue to dream dreams.

This book is also dedicated to the Cancer Support Community in Knoxville, TN whose mission is to ensure that all people impacted by cancer are empowered by knowledge, strengthened by action and sustained by community.

Table of Contents

<u>Foreword</u>

Loris Malaguzzi wrote the following: "Learning and teaching should not stand on opposite banks and just watch the river flow by; instead, they should embark together on a journey down the water. Through an active, reciprocal exchange, teaching can strengthen learning how to learn."

Learning should be a collaborative effort between professor and student. This book is a result of such an effort at the highest level between Dr. Daryl Green and Ms. Noriko Chapman during their time together in the Lincoln Memorial University's Master of Business Administration program. Congratulations to you both on your work that will surely touch and inspire others to do more than they ever thought possible.

-Dr. Jack McCann, Dean of the Lincoln Memorial University School of Business, Harrogate, TN

Acknowledgements

God gave me a second chance!

In 2009 after being diagnosed with cancer, I was devastated by the life threatening disease and unknown future. A year later I have survived and gained my health back for a second chance at life. It's because of the support given by my sister, family, friends, co-workers, neighbors, church members and even the people I didn't know then who reminded me to stay positive and strong and prayed for my health. Otherwise, I would not be back at work or here at Lincoln Memorial University pursuing an MBA. I thank God for giving me an opportunity to know Dr. Daryl Green who challenged and encouraged students to gain wisdom and publish books. This book is an opportunity for me to document the time when I was able to work with such dedicated staff and hard-working clients at Tennessee Rehabilitation Center in Maryville, TN. Through the experience, I hoped to provide some tools and knowledge to help more individuals with disability to seek successful long-term employment as "Second Chance." My appreciation to Deborah Quillen is enormous. I greatly thank my employer, Denso Manufacturing, TN for their full support on my project and for the opportunity to obtain higher education. At last I'm truly thankful for my two beautiful boys, Seth and Zane who always give me love and encouragement and have been willing to adjust to my busy schedule.

Best Wishes,

Noriko

For I know the thoughts that I think toward you, says the Lord, thoughts of peace and not of evil to give you a future and a hope.

(Jeremiah 29:11)

Preface

Dr. Daryl D. Green

My goal is to always prepare my students for the future. As 15 million people are currently unemployed in America, there is no certainty what the future holds. While at Lincoln Memorial University, I have had the honor to lecture to a group of very bright students. I love to challenge and press them toward excellence. While many professors require their graduate students to write research papers, I challenge them to transform the world with their research. I encourage them to publish a book based on their research. Unfortunately, few students take the time to develop their excellence. Most people only want to survive my class. I have never written with any of my students. Writing a book requires a lot of work and energy. In fact, co-authoring a book with someone can be stressful because it is often a one sided affair. Yet, I saw something special in Noriko Chapman. She took her class project seriously. She worked diligently with her client. I could tell she was passionate about her subject. After the course was over, I encouraged her to finalize her project in a paperback format (she turned in an e-book). I sent her instructions; she would comply. It was clear that Noriko had a special talent in writing. Therefore, I agreed to work on this project with her. I believe that God has a special purpose for each of us. Therefore, I do hope it will bless millions of people across the world.

Noriko Chapman

A challenge.

I took Dr. Green's challenge as an opportunity to step up and learn something new. Even if I would fall short, I could learn something from my own mistakes. Nothing to lose. It was more convenient to walk away from the challenge, but now I am glad that I took the challenge to heart.

Then God unfolded many opportunities.

I learned many nonprofit organizations are often limited to obtain additional resources to review the effectiveness and efficiency of their operations. The staff is usually occupied with meeting their primary missions and do not have time to step away from their daily operations to review and make some operational improvements. A lot of people can benefit from the services in the community if the organizations can increase the capacity to accommodate them. Our study is just the first step in recognizing the needs. It is hoped that we will find more volunteers engaged in activities like ours. Additionally, a partial profit from the book sales will be donated to the Maryville Tennessee Rehabilitation Center to support their operation.

Second Chance will provide nonprofit organizations with operations management tools to make them more efficient and better equipped to assist their clients and constituents in meeting their needs. Through my eyes as a new MBA student, readers will be taken on a magical journey of overcoming difficult situations in operations management and also my life.

Introduction

A small car part started this journey.

God uses different people and life events to guide us through life's journey. One day an MBA project and a small car part emerged. The opportunity uncovered a vocational rehabilitation center where individuals with disabilities were trying to learn work skills and find opportunities for gainful employment. The Center is designed to help individuals learn work skills and gain confidence and finally find long-term employment. There are many dedicated people involved to fund the operations, organize the program or work with trainees day to day with passion and patience.

An MBA project called the Real-World Application (RWA) instructed by Dr. Green at Lincoln Memorial University in his Operations Management and Quantitative Analysis class was designed for students to learn through the application of actual operations problems. His expectation was for students to focus on an operational problem in an actual, preferably in a local, nonprofit organization requiring at least 80 hours of effort. The small car part mistakenly packaged wrong captured Noriko's attention to pursue the problem solving and improving the operations to avoid any reoccurrence. This book is based on a true story. Some of the characters have been renamed to protect their privacy and business propertied information. What Noriko encountered was more than consulting operational problems. There was the purpose driven program needing more support from the community and its recognition. The program needed different aspects of support varying from job replacements to an operational improvement to provide suitable training tools to clients.

Noriko realized that she could not assist with all the problems but focused on operational issues in manufacturing settings where she was most familiar.

In addition, there is an urgent need for expanding the capacity to serve the larger population. Based on the research data from the 2007 American Community Survey, approximately 12.8% of Americans between the ages of 21 and 64 have a disability. In Fiscal Year 2009, the Division of Rehabilitation Services provided services to 30,289 individuals in Tennessee and 27,932 individuals met the eligibility criteria of the program. It is projected that 30,000 individuals will receive services and that 27,000 individuals will meet the eligibility criteria of the program and receive services during Fiscal Year 2011[1].

Second Chance provides nonprofit organizations with information about how to use operations management tools to make them more efficient and better equipped to assist their clients and constituents in meeting their needs. Nonprofit organizations like for profit organizations must find innovative ways to compete with others. This includes competing on several dimensions which are (a) cost or price, (b) quality, (c) speed, (d) delivery reliability, and (e) coping with change (Figure 1).

---

[1] Tennessee Division of Rehabilitation Services State Plan for Fiscal Year 2011 (Draft) by Tennessee Department of Human Services

Figure 1 Organization's Competitive Dimensions

Through Noriko's eyes as an MBA student, readers will be taken on a magical journey of overcoming a difficult situation in operations management and my life. Nonprofit managers will benefit in the following ways:

• Learn how to navigate operations management as it relates to nonprofit organizations.

• Gain greater confidence in your ability to apply these concepts to your own problems and issues.

• Discover how to break from your own limitations by breaking the barriers of your self-doubt.

An MBA professor and an MBA student found the opportunity to pursue the project. Both knew everything would come all together without manipulating every single detail if it is God's intention. The timing was perfect. If it is God's will, the timing is always right without coordinating it. We need to find it and jump in. It may take more time and energy than anticipated to yield the fruit of accomplishment. But it is truly worth it!

"Live as if you were to die tomorrow. Learn as if you were to live forever."

\- Mahatma Gandhi

Chapter 1

Dream is Over

"Noriko, I'm very sorry... I don't have good news for you. You have cancer. It's very aggressive," said Dr. Wilson after carefully closing a door and sliding her chair closer to me.

"What did I just hear?" I was confused.

"I will recommend you a very good oncologist in Knoxville. Trust me he will take good care of you." She took my hands and softly held them.

"Will I be alive when my children are graduating from high school? Who is going to take care of them if something happens to me? How about my dreams I've been chasing?" I felt fear, trapped, lost, anxious, and alone.

I cannot remember how I drove myself back from the doctor's office to work. It was still raining hard after the severe thunderstorm. Looking outside from my office window, I wiped tears again, finally picked up a phone and slowly dialed.

"Dr. Dillon, this is Noriko Chapman."

"Hi."

"I'm calling to cancel my 5:30pm appointment with you this evening."

"Should we reschedule it?" asked Dr. Dillon nicely.

"No, I probably cannot. I won't be able to start MBA classes because of my serious health issue. I'm sorry," I was barely able to finish the conversation.

"I understood, but the enrollment is valid through spring semester. Keep it in your mind."

"Thank you. I will let you know when I'm ready," I said to Dr. Dillon even though I had no idea when I would be ready or if I would be ever able to resume a normal life.

Operation Management Challenges in Nonprofit Organizations

With shrinking funds for programs and a more competitive environment, nonprofit organizations will need to rethink their corporate strategies for future success. This reality means managing their operations more efficiently and shifting their traditional thinking to a more entrepreneurial approach. Today's businesses have built elaborate systems for better efficiency and effectiveness.

Of course, they are driven by the quest for more profitability. Operations management (OM) has been a vital instrument in the pursuit of greater productivity. OM includes planning, coordinating, and executing all activities that create goods and services[2]. This concept goes by many names including production, supply chain management, and engineering and production systems. In the past, the major emphasis was centered on manufacturing processes. Times have changed. Today, OM provides businesses with methods to effectively produce and distribute goods and services to customers. Robert Jacobs, Richard Chase, and Nicholas Aquilano, authors of Operations & Supply Management, suggest that implementing OM assists organizations to be more competitive: "Compared with most of the other ways managers try to stimulate growth – technology investments, acquisitions, and major market campaigns, for example – innovations in operations are relatively reliable and low cost."[3] OM uses analytical thinking to deal with operational issues.

---

[2] Operations Management by Jae Shim and Joel Siegel

[3] Operations & Supply Management by Robert Jacobs, Richard Chase, and Nicholas Aquilana

Therefore, the OM concept is related to the process-oriented analysis of organizational systems.

Today's managers have placed greater focus on Lean Manufacturing, TQM, Six-Sigma Quality, and Supply Chain Manufacturing. Some of the OM tools include time studies, quantitative analysis, and plant design. Yet, OM is not only for manufacturing. In fact, operational effectiveness speaks to the needs of all organizations seeking great efficiencies.

However, service organizations are different from manufacturing operations. In general, there is a higher degree of customer contact in the operations which makes it more difficult to control the overall processes. Like most service organizations, nonprofit organizations have a great need for increased effectiveness in their processes. Nonprofit organizations are different from traditional organizations and require careful considerations in implementing OM processes. Nonprofit organizations exist for the common good of others. Their purpose is often to meet one or more needs in a community. This can include educational or charitable reasons. Public charities account for over 60% of all registered nonprofit organizations.

However, private organizations are also vital. According to the Giving USA Foundation in 2007, private charities contributions reached over $295 billion in 2006[4].

Unlike businesses that are driven primarily by profit, nonprofits use any monies earned to be put back into the organization to cover their own expenses, operations, and programs.

---

[4] "Non-profit market," by Closerware

In 2005, there will be approximately 1.4 million nonprofit organizations registered to the IRS[5]. The majority of nonprofits depend on volunteers at various levels. In fact, 74% of all public charities and 83% of all foundations are small; they have less than $500,000 in expenses and limited staff[6].

Most nonprofits limit their continual resources to fully utilize modern management tools or advanced technology. They are often influenced by their stakeholders that include clients, board, committees, government officials, community leaders, staff, and volunteers[7]. In general, nonprofit operations are organized into major functions; these functions are usually centered around central administration and programs[8]. In fact, most are forced to rely upon low-end technologies and outdated practices. Therefore, leadership becomes key in implementing operational changes. Nonprofit leaders must be able and willing to provide staff with vision, skill, and sufficient resources to accomplish the organization's mission[9].

The Tennessee Vocational Rehabilitation is one of these nonprofit organizations looking for more operational effectiveness in the future.

---

[5] "Non-profit market," by Closerware

[6] "Non-profit market," by Closerware

[7] "Basic overview of nonprofit organizations," by Carter McNamara

[8] "Basic overview of nonprofit organizations," by Carter McNamara

[9] "Basic overview of nonprofit organizations," by Carter McNamara

Tennessee Vocational Rehabilitation is a federal and state-funded program run by the Tennessee Department of Human Services Division of Rehabilitation Services to assist individuals of work age with physical and/or mental disabilities to compete successfully with others in earning a livelihood. [10]

Community Tennessee Rehabilitation Centers (TRCs) are designed to provide special emphasis programs at seventeen locations throughout Tennessee. Based on the 2011 state plan by The State Rehabilitation Council who works in partnership with the Division of Rehabilitation Services, the council believes many good things are happening with Vocational Rehabilitation in Tennessee. However, there is much room for improvement if the division is going to enable citizens with disabilities to maximize their potential[11].

The Maryville Center is one of the non-profit organizations funded by the Federal Government, Blount County, City of Maryville, and City of Alcoa, that offers comprehensive vocational evaluation services, employee development services, job readiness training and job placement.

The Maryville Center was established in August 1966[12]. Sharon Davis, the Center secretary explains that the center has experienced the sales fluctuations due to the area economy during the 44 years of operation.

---

[10] Human Services – About Us by Tennessee Department of Human Services

[11] Tennessee Division of Rehabilitation Services State Plan for Fiscal Year 2011(Draft) by Tennessee Department of Human Services

[12] Interview with Sharon Davis

Some jobs became obsolete from the established contract vendors due to the jobs being conducted in-house with the companies. In 2009, the Maryville TRC was ranked at eighth in contract sales when the Columbia TRC achieved the largest sales in Tennessee [13]. Its mission is to provide services that help lead individuals who have a physical and/or mental disability to employment and are designed to meet individual needs. Individuals who are eligible:

• Have a physical or mental disability that constitutes or results in a substantial impediment to employment.

• Can benefit from the vocational rehabilitation services to reach an employment outcome.

• Require the vocational rehabilitation services to prepare for, obtain, keep or regain employment.

• Social Security Disability Insurance (SSDI) or Supplemental Security Income (SSI) recipients are presumed eligible for services if intending to secure employment [14].

This nonprofit study focuses on the production capacity, client allocation, productivity improvement, and quality control while industry outsourcing jobs are fully utilized to train clients at the TRC Maryville location.

---

[13] Interview with Sharon Davis

[14] Interview with Sharon Davis

"Courage is the discovery that you may not win, and trying when you know you can lose." - Tom Krause

Chapter 2

Later Years

On a hot summer day in August, I finally arrived at the plant at 8:10am after dropping off two sons at city schools. My younger son had left his homework at home, and we had to drive back to the house and then turn around to get back to school. Why didn't he have everything in his backpack last night?

My next meeting was at 8:30am. I was in a hurry for the daily meeting in 10 minutes. As I was walking through my office, I found a box of parts sitting unusually on my desk. "What is that box?" I carefully looked at the parts in the black box and found a note saying "Noriko, Bad parts. Can you fix them? Thanks, Bill." The defective parts appeared to be from the vocational center, two blocks away from our plant.

"Doesn't everyone know I have hundreds of other things to take care of? God, is it going to be one of those bad days?" I murmured.

I was getting very frustrated. It should be such a simple operation to pack 20 parts in a tube in the same direction. The wrong part could have caused machine jam and then in a worst case a production downtime. I decided to go to the source and wanted to find out the reason for the part being packed in a wrong orientation.

After I arrived at the center, it was not hard to find out the cause of the quality problem.

The Economic Crisis

The current economic crisis frightens most nonprofit executives. And what if the situation does not get better? Economic turbulence has interrupted our pursuit of liberty and happiness. With a weak job growth, many U.S. jobs will continue to be outsourced globally or automated through technology. Therefore, organizations are very careful of their investments. In the wake of nonprofit scandals in America, corporate executives are more skeptical of nonprofit organizations. With the passage of the Sarbanes-Oxley Act of 2002, the government has signaled that nonprofit organizations will no longer be able to fly under the radar of society.[15] However, they are not alone in scrutinizing nonprofits. Board of directors, donors, government agencies, foundations, and the general public are concerned about how nonprofit organizations operate and behave in society. With the economic crisis and increased scrutiny, nonprofit organizations face a difficult time with sustainability due to financial issues. Fundraising and grants are a major source of funding for most nonprofit organizations. Devolution is a word that frightens many nonprofits. It relates to the strong trend of cutbacks by government agencies to reduce their funding to nonprofit organizations.[16]

---

[15] "More than 900 nonprofit professionals take steps to improve accountability," by Blackbaud

[16] Basic overview of nonprofit organizations," by Carter McNamara

According to Campaign Consultation, Inc. in 2003, the federal government has reduced domestic spending for human service items.[17] Consequently, nonprofit organizations find themselves in a fierce battle with each other for limited government funding. Therefore, the economic crisis will drive new approaches to the nonprofit market.

In order to support the TRC in Maryville, Tennessee, Noriko analyzed the client population, the center capacity, current job, and the job allocation method to determine how efficiently and effectively the Center was operating. This study was conducted between October 10th and November 30th, 2010. While the center has been pleased with the increasing number of referrals by approximately 70% from 169 applicants in 2005 - 2006 to 287 applicants in 2008 - 2009, they are also adjusting the operations to the recovering economy and increasing volumes. In fact, on November 1st the Center developed an additional contract with a nearby stationery company. After the 2008 recession, there are more outsourced job opportunities already requested by the companies in the community. In order to supply good quality parts on time to the customers, the resources and their capabilities need to be evaluated periodically and are fully utilized. The evaluation is crucial before the Center signs new contracts to know if the resources can manage new jobs successfully. Standardization and training are essential to the consistent, quality work for customer satisfaction and future business growth.

---

[17] "Understanding trends impacting nonprofit organizations' budgets," by Campaign Consultation.

The study proposes that TRC utilizes analytical and visual tools to determine accurate capacity and capability to promise and provide high quality, on-time delivery to their customers while maintaining its primary mission of providing "hands-on" real work to train their clients in work skills.

"A relentless barrage of "whys" is the best way to prepare your mind to pierce the clouded veil of thinking caused by the status quo. Use it often." - Shigeo Shingo

Chapter 3

First Day of Class

Finally after leaving my office on a hectic day, I was driving to Lincoln Memorial University campus for the first day of MBA 511 Operations Management and Supply Chain class.

At the end of the first lecture, Dr. Green explained about the Real World Application (RWA) project. An 80-hour work week on the top of five case studies, weekly blogs, and a mid-term exam! I didn't know if I could handle all the school load between my busy work schedule and children's schedule. I should not be stressed out over school. I had to take care of my health also.

"God, help me!" The RWA weighed 1/3 of the grade, and it had to be something I was familiar with and would keep me interested throughout the entire semester.

"How about the vocational center I visited yesterday?" It was a non-profit organization as he encouraged students to help. We had to fix the problem anyway for my company. It may not be a bad idea.

Case Study Overview

Vocational evaluation helps clients identify their work interests and abilities. One of the objectives of Tennessee Rehabilitation Center (TRC) is to search and gain business opportunities in the community to secure enough, suitable work for clients. TRC offers a variety of services to area businesses through industry outsourcing opportunities. The Center supports the area businesses to receive quality, timely and cost effective services by dedicated workforce with warehouse space, loading docks and forklifts. The jobs vary from small assembly, disassembly, bagging, mailings, quality, control, and packing.

Twenty-two clients a month on average are trained at the Maryville Center in an approximately 15,000 square feet plant. As of October 10th, 2010, seventeen clients were enrolled in the employee development workshop program during the time this study was conducted.[18] The average training length is four months. Some clients may stay with the Center for up to one year to complete their trainings. Seven out of the seventeen clients are seniors from high school special education classes in Maryville and Alcoa, Tennessee. Holmes notes that the TRC has developed strong relationships with high school teachers and special educators across the state. The TRC continues to strengthen relationships and partnerships with the high schools to better serve potential and eligible clients with disabilities.[19]

---

[18] Interview with Deborah Quillen

[19] Outcomes Management and Strategic Planning Report By David Holmes

The Center obtains a special minimum wage certificate to compensate clients for the work accomplished while being trained. The U.S. Department of Labor certifies individuals whose earning or productive capacity is impaired by a physical or mental disability, including those related to age or injury may be paid sub-minimum wages pursuant to a certificate issued by the Secretary of Labor. Employment at less than the minimum wage is authorized to prevent curtailment of opportunities for employment for workers with disabilities based on the Fair Labor Standards Act (2009).

The high school students are transported by the city school buses. Some adults use the East Tennessee Human Resource Agency (ETHRA) transportation. Both transportation methods are helpful for the Center staff to expect the time the clients arrive and leave the Center.[20]

The staff consists of six positions as the organizational chart shows in Figure 2. The current jobs are outsourced to the center mainly by two companies: an automotive components company in the same industrial park and a nearby stationery company a few miles away from the Center. The jobs consist of five different parts requiring such operations as re-packing, packaging and a simple sub-assembly process. The automotive components company provides a daily truck to pick up finished goods and drop off components. Four operations are time-sensitive jobs to satisfy daily requirements as the company runs under the just-in-time operation system.

---

[20] Interview with Lisa Burchfield

There are some jobs that are not time-sensitive which can be processed only when the manning is sufficient.

Clients are paid by the number of pieces completed and summed up to bi-weekly paychecks. The piece prices range approximately from $0.01 to $0.30. The typical operation hours are 8:30am - 2:30pm for six hours including two 10-minute breaks and a half-hour lunch. For instance, adults may take home approximately $38 - $215 bi-weekly while high school students may earn $39 - 120 bi-weekly. The Daily Time and Production Sheet is a current tool that records the daily outputs of each client and is designed for supervisors to review. It is designed to keep records of weekly outputs and signed by both client and staff before submitting to the center manager to sum up to bi-weekly paychecks. In addition, it is important to understand that the majority of the adult population receives SSDI or SSI. Therefore, the income from the TRC training is supplemental, and the clients do not have to rely on it for making a living. [21]

The following elements are key attributes for the operations:

> **Inputs:** Services including diagnosis, counseling & guidance, treatment, training, maintenance & transportation, transition services from school to work, personal care assistance program, independent living services, assistive technology, supported employment, job placement and post-employment services.

---

[21] Interview with Deborah Quillen

Outputs: Clients who prepare for employment which can lead to meaningful and satisfying careers and centers that can continue to grow and provide the well-designed services to future clients.

The main constraint of the TRC operations is the population fluctuations due to:

• Individual capabilities due to disabilities;

• Short-term employment since the employment is a part of training programs;

• The number of clients referred to the TRC is unpredictable.

In addition, the logical converse of funding being limited and uncertain is the fact that demands for public human and rehabilitation services is higher than ever before.[22]

TRC is one of the publicly funded human service and rehabilitation services facing the dilemma of improving productivity among people with disabilities.

---

[22] Work by Allen Lewis

"It is not enough to do your best; you must know what to do, and then do your best." - W. Edwards Deming

Chapter 4

A Project Meant to Be

"Don, I need your permission to pursue this project," I explained the scope of the RWA project to our company director who was allowing me to use our company related materials.

"It's a win-win situation. While you are helping the center, you are helping our company." Don continued, "This is a perfect project for you. You deal with customer fluctuations daily. It's a little different kind of fluctuation, but you are already used to the dynamic operation."

"Yes, Don. I've dealt with customer order fluctuations for many years. Since I took this new responsibility working with suppliers almost 3 months ago, I've been facing different challenges. I wouldn't be involved with this supplier problem unless I got the responsibility," I answered and continued.

"I've got an idea. Can you let me use our product to show how the part is important to run the machine and complete the assembly? It will be so much easier for trainees to see and understand the importance of their job to keep us with good quality."

"This project must be designed just for you. You've got my full support!" Don smiled at me.

Case Study Analysis

Several analyses were conducted to review how the center operated with its capacity, client allocation, productivity improvement and quality control.

1. Organizational Structure – TN Rehabilitation Center (Maryville Location)

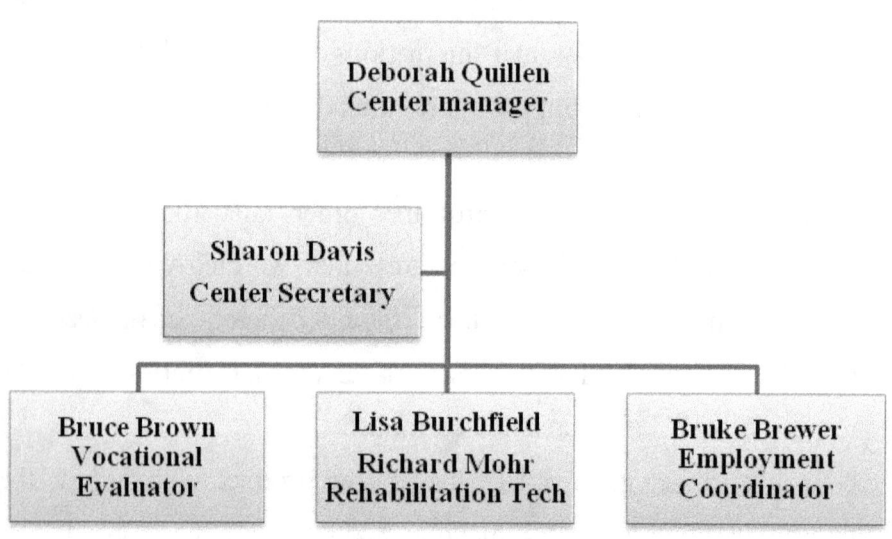

Figure 2 Organization Chart – TN Rehabilitation Center, Maryville Location

Deborah Quillen has been a center manager for six years after serving as a rehabilitation counselor for many years. Lisa Burchfield and Richard Mohr work daily with clients and are in charge of operations and job assignments while monitoring and evaluating each client's job performance. Both rehabilitation technicians have excellent manufacturing experience in standard business settings.

2. Employment Process

During the application and evaluation process, 10 - 12 clients at monthly average are accepted by the center for the training or other DRS services. As the result of personalizing training programs, approximately 4 - 5 clients monthly are referred to the work adjustment training.[23] Applicants are reviewed for acceptance or denial through the system illustrated by Figure 3.[24]

The TRC employee development program is just one service offered for training to the clients. Other clients may be referred to other disability rehabilitation programs such as college, on-the-job training, vocational and technical training. In 2009, 27 clients entered the Maryville Center when 58 clients were referred to the Center. After the individualized training, 27 clients were placed in successful employment.[25]

The information about specific disabilities as shown in Figure 4 is crucial for counselors and rehabilitation technicians to provide appropriate services to their clients. For instance, Traumatic Brain Injury (TBI) is a complex disability due to the nature of the injuries that cause destruction of brain tissues. Most common causes of injury are rapid deceleration accidents such as automobile or motorcycle accidents.[26]

---

[23] Interview with Bruce Brown

[24] Interview with Deborah Quillen

[25] Interview with Deborah Quillen

[26] The Disability Handbook by Jason Andrew

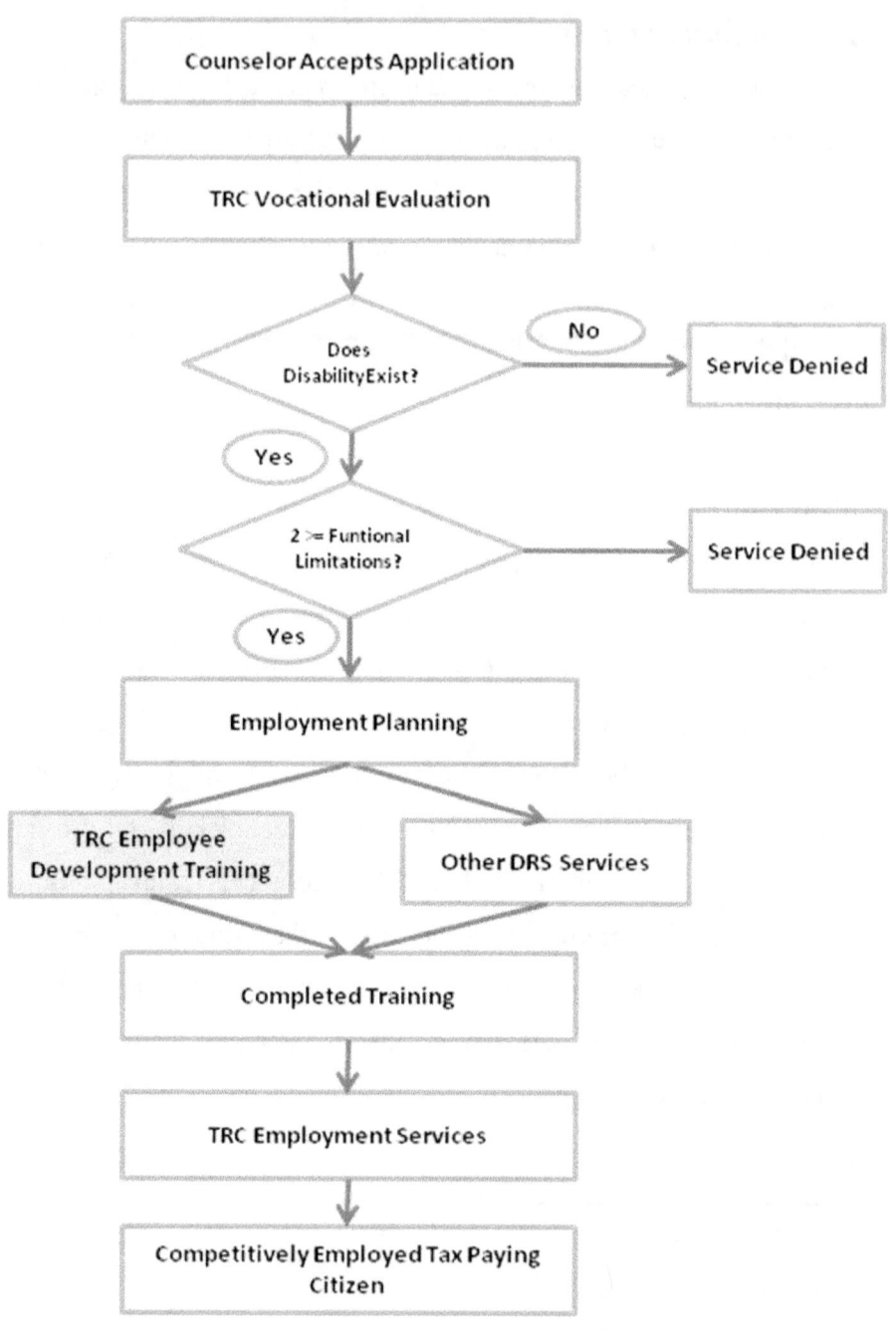

Figure 3 Service Flow for an Individual with Disability Seeking Employment

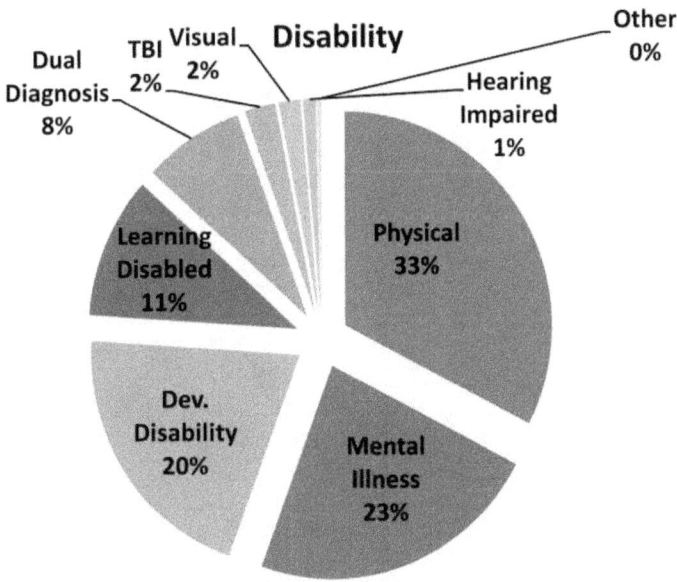

Figure 4 Disability Categories – TRC Maryville Location, 2009

Clients with TBI may have been successfully employed before the accidents but become unable to maintain their previous jobs. The training center provides a comprehensive vocational assessment to evaluate and provide adequate jobs for each client.

"We are what we repeatedly do. Excellence, then, is not an act, but habit." - Aristotle

Chapter 5

God Sent Me to This Center

On a sunny fall day, Jane was taking an afternoon break outside the center. All the daily requirements were met for the day. A milk-run truck already picked up the repacked parts.

"Jane, I need a little more information for my paper," as I finally found Jane outside and sat down with her.

"By the way, I didn't see the adult clients but only Eric inside," I was a little puzzled.

Jane answered, "Eric is waiting for a return ride by ETHRA. High school students left in the morning, and everyone else left for the day."

I questioned, "So was all the work done for today?"

"Yes, we don't have enough work to keep everyone busy…"

I quickly commented, "That justifies my time study. Do you remember when I was figuring out the cycle time and then calculated it in work volumes the other day? We can take more work. Jane, we've got to find right jobs for them!"

Jane looked at me and said, "Hey, I heard that you've invited your president to our Thanksgiving luncheon as a guest."

"Oh, he is such a manufacturing oriented person. I thought he would love to see this center and maybe give us some advice about operations," I smiled back at Jane.

"Noriko, it never happened to us. You know what? God must have sent you to the center."

My memory traveled back to a year before in September.

My oncologist told me that the cancer cell invasion was amazingly so little that I didn't have to take any radiation or chemotherapy treatments after the second surgery. Angela was one of my friends who were thrilled by the good news.

She soon responded after the news was delivered, "Noriko, God is not finished with you yet. He has a special mission for you." It got stuck in my mind and I have been searching for the answer since then.

"Is this project one of the special missions I'm supposed to accomplish by God's will?"

DMTN President, Van Saka, visits the Tennessee Rehabilitation Center of Blount County

Case Study Findings

After the review of the center's operating systems, several issues emerged. First, the center's accountability relies on the quality of jobs. Consistent, high quality is a key to maintain the current vendor contracts and expand to new contract opportunities and new customers. Secondly, the center deals with the fluctuations of client population. The issues are discussed in the following subsections.

1. Operational Challenges

On August 18, the center was notified of one of the FINs; an electronic component was packed in a wrong orientation which could have caused a machine jam and production stop to the customer. Also the outside of tubes were damp. It is one of the challenges of TRC to maintain consistent quality work since their labor source is on a temporary basis and not a standardized workforce due to the population with disabilities. The other problem is to foresee the capacity. TRC is designed to employ clients to adjust and train in work skills in work environment and find suitable, long-term employment. Due to the population fluctuation, the center has been turning down additional business opportunities because of the fear of commitment.

There were two operation problems concerning the quality. One of the problems was the FIN packaged in a wrong orientation in a tube. The center soon added an additional person to perform the second inspection (Figure 5).

Figure 5 FIN Packaging Operations

The additional inspection required a person and increased the cycle time but at very minimum. The center also added an inspection tag with the client's name for each box before tubes are boxed at the final staging. The tag helps clients hold the accountability while it also can help identify a responsible inspector when defect parts are found.

The other problem involved the sub-assembly process of two automotive components. Clients put one of each component together to make a bag of 300 pieces of sub-assembled parts before sending them back to the customer. The lot size of rubber caps was 500 pieces while the bag quantity of copper connectors was 300 pieces. Some clients are not capable of counting correctly. Due to the lot size inconsistency, 200 pieces of rubber caps were always left out and applied to a next batch. If the rubber lot size could be changed to 300 pieces, both components would be equally depleted after the completion of 300 sub-assembled parts. This is one good example of using a Poka-Yoke mistake proof to control and assure good quality even for anyone who can count. If they find any parts left on a table after completing a bag of 300 parts, it should be reported as abnormal. The next step should be a sorting to find parts missing components. To accommodate the Center's request, the company was able to negotiate with their rubber cap supplier to reduce the bag quantity from 500 pieces to 300 pieces.

In addition, the Center manager emphasizes that the primary challenge in training individuals with disabilities is not the barrier of the disability but maintaining motivation in the client to pursue employment and continue to pursue goals. The challenge is to motivate clients to maintain jobs and find interests in their jobs.[27] Many clients are somewhat isolated in the society, and some may never have worked in the past. It is a challenge for those who have never worked to be exposed to work experiences outside of their daily life and find interests in employment.

2. Operational Constraints

The employment situation is different from normal business practices because the Center is designed to discharge the best workers to pursue community employment.[28] Due to the inconsistent work population, an overloaded business may cause quality and delivery issues, which may lessen future business opportunities. The Center has to maintain a careful labor population assessment periodically and a fine balance between workload and clients' capability.

---

[27] Interview with Deborah Quillen

[28] Interview with Lisa Burchfield

Five major constraints are identified as below:

1. Unique population concerning the following performance criteria:

    a. Attendance/Punctuality;

    b. Hygiene/Appearance;

    c. Staying on task;

    d. Follows instructions;

    e. Works independently;

    f. Cooperation with supervisors, co-workers, and team;

    g. Safety practices;

    h. Work tolerance;

    i. Work speed and quality;

    j. Work related judgment/response to corrections;

    k. Work related skills, independent living, academic and job readiness.

2. Short-term employment (average at 4 months);

3. Forecast the number of clients referred to the center;

4. Not enough work to maintain consistent work hours for clients in the training program;

5. Deviated work hours due to supplemental trainings or different work days from customer's work schedule due to observing national holidays.

	Description	Qty/min	Cycle Time (seconds)	Daily Volume	Hours/Day	Time Sensitive?
CURRENT	MAGNETS (Blue Tray)	42	1.4	20800	8.25	YES
	MAGNETS (White Tray)	42	1.4	1440	0.57	YES
	COPPER CONNECTOR					
	RUBBER CAP TERMINAL	4	15.0	2000	4.09	YES
	METAL FIN	5	12.0	4000	13.33	YES
	Time-Sensitive Job Total Hours Required				26.25	Hours/day
	PEN TIPS	50	1.2	300,000	100.00	NO
FUTURE	FELT TIPS					NO
	DIODE (sorting dropped parts)			50,000/Month		NO

Table 1   Job Time Study and Requirement Matrix

The current work accumulates to 26.25 hours per day as shown in Table 1 while 186.50 weekly work hours or the daily average of 37.30 hours are available as calculated in Table 2. High school students are assigned to 8:45am - 11:30am operation hours daily. However, some adults have been dismissed early due to the light workload in the afternoons. The Center has more than enough capacity for the current contract work (Figure 6).

Weekly Schedule (as of 11/8/10)

Client	MON	TUE	WED	THU	FRI	TOTAL
A	2.25	2.25	2.25	2.25	2.25	11.25
B	2.25	2.25	2.25	2.25	2.25	11.25
C	2.25	2.25	2.25	2.25	2.25	11.25
D	2.25	2.25	2.25	2.25	2.25	11.25
E	2.25	2.25	2.25	2.25	2.25	11.25
F	2.25	2.25	2.25	2.25	2.25	11.25
G	2.25	2.25	2.25	2.25	2.25	11.25
H	2.25	2.25	2.25	2.25	2.25	11.25
I	3.00	3.00	3.00	3.00	3.00	15.00
J	4.50	0.00	0.00	4.50	0.00	9.00
K	3.00	3.00	3.00	0.00	0.00	9.00
L	3.00	3.00	3.00	3.00	0.00	12.00
M	4.50	4.50	4.50	4.50	0.00	18.00
N	5.00	5.00	5.00	5.00	0.00	20.00
O	0.00	4.50	4.50	4.50	0.00	13.50
	41.00	41.00	41.00	42.50	21.00	**186.50**

Lunch/Breaks and Daily 30min Set Up/Clean Up Excluded

Table 2 Weekly Client Schedule

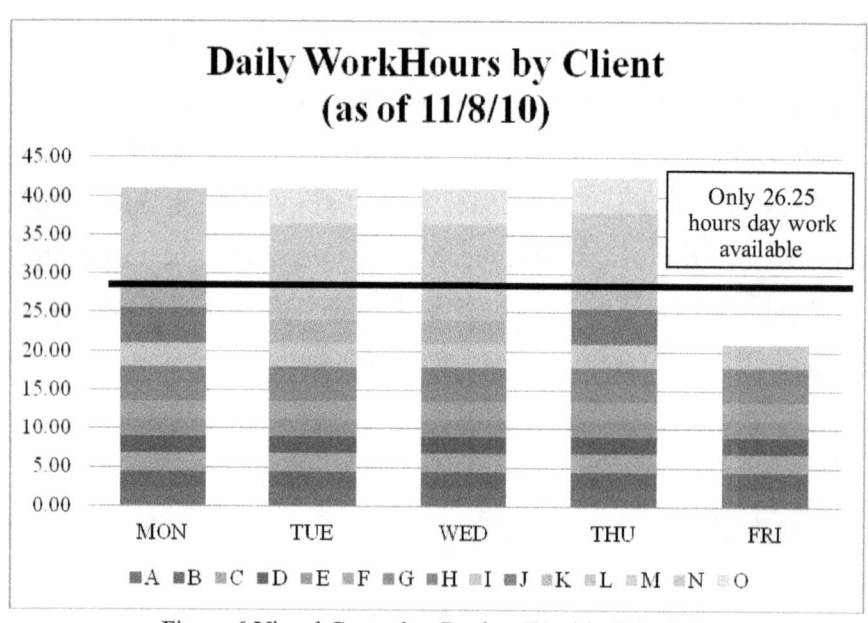

Figure 6 Visual Control to Review Weekly Schedule

Even though absenteeism or call-ins are their main concerns, the Center has enough capacity to operate and meet customers' requirements as long as the management keeps track of daily or weekly work hours and know when to react quickly by prioritizing such as setting aside the non time-sensitive jobs. Therefore, obtaining non time-sensitive jobs is one way to absorb those labor fluctuations. An example of a non time-sensitive job may be a large bulk of parts to be sorted and tested to send back to the customer whenever they can be processed. Thus, the customer does not expect the parts to be delivered in a timely manner. It is strongly recommended that the center confirms the customers work schedule periodically such as daily operation hours, summer shutdowns and holidays. When the Center shuts down in order to observe national holidays and school closings customers do not, they need to adjust the production schedule to produce and deliver ahead to meet on-time deliveries.

"Improvement usually means doing something that we have never done before." - Shigeo Shingo

Chapter 6

Opportunities Found in Problems

"I had no idea the Center was located only a block away from our facility," President Saka said while we were taking a plant tour at the Center.

"It always makes me appreciative when I see people with disabilities working hard and having pride in their own jobs. It's an eye opener. In Japan, I used to visit Denso Taiyo[29] and got involved with their Kaizen (continuous improvement) activities as a Kaizen Circle judge. They always had great ideas that we never thought of. It amazed us."

"Isn't that Denso's subsidiary that employs 77 handicapped people and made about US$70 Millions in 2009 sales[30]?" I replied.

"Yeah, Taiyo actually set up assembly lines and makes fully assembled finished goods to ship directly to customers. I've noticed here the jobs are individual tasks not a team task....." President Saka said.

"Yes, these trainees are paid by pieces. That's one of the reasons the Center needs to set up the work processes individually so that trainees and supervisors can keep track of yields," I added.

"President Saka, unfortunately the Center doesn't have enough work to keep seventeen trainees busy," I hesitantly brought up a concern.

---

[29] Company Profile by Denso Taiyo Co.,LTD.

[30] Company Profile by Denso Taiyo Co.,LTD.

"Oh, surely there are some jobs available for them. Don't we have daily milk-run trucks between Maryville and Athens Plants?"

"Yes, sir," I quickly replied.

"For them it's important to learn how to keep up with assembly speed with other team members. The work skill will be beneficial when they get jobs in the real world. Let's look at some possible work for them!"

Noriko Chapman and Deborah Quillen collaborate to give the Tennessee Rehabilitation Center of Blount County a second chance.

Photo by: The Daily Times

Discussion and Implications

The key issue in this case study was how to establish high quality and stable production to maintain and grow business for the Center while providing adequate and a variety of work to their clients. The first step to evaluate the quality is to analyze customer complaints and identify the root causes of problems. It helps identify problems as client capability, motivation issues or system issues. Maintaining the high quality will become a marketing tool to seek other jobs in the community. Recently the Center has been approached to obtain an ISO certificate or Six Sigma to be eligible for some government contracted work.

The second recommendation is to evaluate the capacity along with the capability of existing workforce if the Center needs to adjust work hours or bring more clients to meet customer requirements. Noriko strongly encouraged that the Center maintains the jobs that are time-sensitive and non time-sensitive in order to absorb manpower fluctuations due to absenteeism, and clients experience level. It is also recommended for flexible manning by training clients on all different tasks as long as the limitations of their disabilities do not keep them from doing the tasks. The training record shown as Figure 7, demonstrates the training status of each client. Each pie represents the progress of different jobs by each client. The pie slices are divided into four training stages. The first stage is to receive the initial training. The client requires guidance and support. The second stage is to receive basic training. A client can perform the job without supervision.

Third, the client can perform to standard level, which is equal to 100% compliance to the standardized work. At last the client can train other clients. The training record can be reviewed and updated weekly. It is recommended to post it where clients and staff can see the progress. It also can be a tool to motivate clients whose goal is to fill in the complete pie.

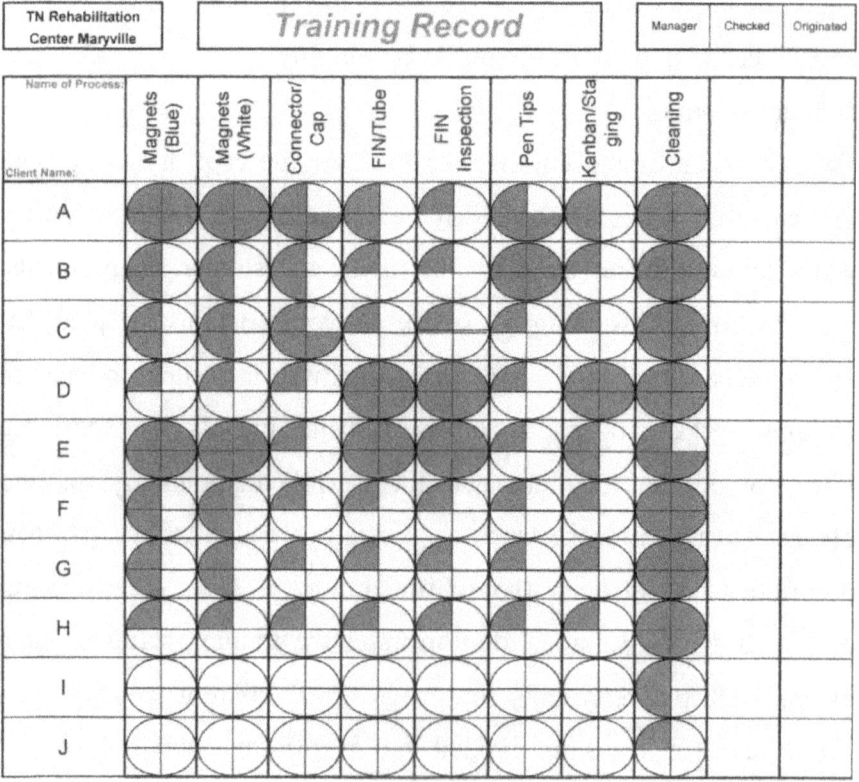

Figure 7 Client Job Training Matrix (Example)

Additionally, it is highly recommended to acknowledge clients when they perform quality jobs above normal expectations. The recognition system can be shared by a center newsletter or a display of good quality work. It helps motivate clients and shares a higher quality standard with other clients.

At last, the tools can be widely introduced to other TRC locations once they are recognized as successful tools at the TRC Maryville Location. Each center manager prepares the annual report. Managers are encouraged to share and benchmark different approaches when they are successfully implemented.[31]

The TRC management desires the annual outcomes management and strategic planning report to be used as a management tool in providing guidance in strategic planning, preparation, and positioning of TRC programs and services for future growth, optimum productivity and maximum effectiveness and efficiency in meeting the needs of clients served.[32]

Furthermore, most of the operations are independently processed by a client from the beginning to the end. It is essential for clients to practice working with others in real manufacturing settings. The teamwork that can be seen on an assembly line is highly recommended to provide another level of training for clients. The quality should not suffer if processes are standardized and are well documented to train clients.

---

[31] Interview with Deborah Quillen

[32] Outcomes Management and Strategic Planning Report By David Holmes

RECOMMENDATIONS

The following recommendations are offered to enhance the Center's operational efficiency to better serve clients and contract vendors effectively over the long term:

1. Control quality to maintain and expand business while providing a good variety of work to the clients. Evaluating customer complaints is the first step to analyze the root cause of problems. It helps identify the problems as client capability, motivation issues or system issues;

2. Evaluate capacity along with the capability of workforce if the center needs to adjust work hours or bring more clients to meet customer requirements;

3. Obtain a good combination of time-sensitive and non time-sensitive jobs;

4. Utilize visual control tools to visualize the progress and problems not only for the staff but also for the clients. The training grid chart (Figure 7) may motivate the clients by viewing their progress on the chart;

5. Establish an inventory control system to keep track of components and finished goods. It becomes more essential as their business grows to manage additional part numbers, volumes and logistical flows;

6. Provide trainings to interest, motivate clients, and be quality conscious;

7. Implement error-proofing system;

8. Standardize work procedures;

9. Benchmark with the other 16 centers in TN;

10. Implement a quality award system to recognize clients who detect defective parts;

11. Obtain quality certificates such as ISO9001 and Six Sigma.

These recommendations were suggested to the Center manager and the rehabilitation technicians. None of the recommendations require capital investment, and they are more likely internal process changes and tool changes. Most recommendations do not require a great amount of time but maintain and update the current system with newly introduced tools. In order to prepare for the quality certification which opens up more job opportunities, some trainings and external support may be required.

"Inconveniences promote creativity."

\- Taiichi Ohno

Conclusion

Final Presentation

"This is it! After this final presentation, no more projects!" I jumped out of bed in the morning and got myself and my kids ready for work and school. I was rehearsing presentation materials over and over while driving them to schools.

"Good luck, Mom!" Zane smiled at me as I was dropping off my son at middle school.

An hour before the final presentation.

I was running out of practicing time while getting anxious to be over with it. Dr. Green told me to bring some energy and passion to convince the audience of my expertise.

"God, help me finish up this presentation with success if this project is truly your plan for me to carry out," I said a quiet prayer in the classroom. At that time, I was lifted up and became confident that He would carry me through the presentation.

Once the presentation started, it was not hard to share something that I knew the best of as Dr. Green said.

I was happy to be giving the closing statements after the 10-minute presentation.

"This project was very rewarding because it's for the people who once were successfully employed but lost their jobs because of injuries by car accidents and would like to regain work skills. Or it's for the women who were abused mentally or physically at some point in their lives and want to gain self-confidence, find jobs, support themselves and find the true meaning of life as their Second Chance…"

I heard the audience applauding and found Dr. Green nodding to me with a smile.

LMU MBA student, Noriko Chapman, and professor team up on book to help the Tennessee Rehabilitation Center of Blount County.
Photo by: Anne Klebenow

With the economic crisis still looming ahead, many organizations are seeking better ways to operate. Nonprofit organizations are not the exception. Many nonprofit organizations lack the ability and knowledge to fully analyze their processes.

Furthermore, this case study demonstrated the benefits of applying operations management techniques to assist a nonprofit organization with being more efficient and effective. That is the case for the Tennessee Rehabilitation Center. The Center is usually the final hope for individuals with disabilities after they exhaust all the possible employment avenues. The Center operates under the unique circumstance that it has to release its best workers for permanent employment replacement outside of the Center.

The Maryville Center operates under a well maintained and safe, clean environment. Currently, the relatively new facility is estimated to be utilized by two thirds. One third is still available for future business growth. The Center staff is extremely motivated and well experienced to serve clients with passion and patience. TRC is not there to make profits but to provide a service for individuals with disabilities to gain long-term, successful employment and greater independence. In order for TRC to provide the work environment as close to the real working situation, clients will be more benefited if the training challenges them with 8-hour, 5-day jobs to adjust closer to the real work settings. The Center has the capacity. If they periodically evaluate the population fluctuation, they should be able to allocate the jobs to clients effectively and efficiently. Even If the workload becomes larger than its capacity, there are multiple ways to absorb the overload.

The Center has the capacity to increase individual work hours to eight hours a day. Some tasks can be divided up more efficiently and lined up on a simple assembly line to increase the productivity while clients can learn how to work with other clients as a team.

Denso Corporation has been actively participating in employment and occupational opportunities for individuals with disabilities since 1978.[33] The special-purpose subsidiary DENSO TAIYO Co., Ltd. currently employs 76 physically challenged people. Denso Corporation is targeting the disabled population to increase from 1.97% in 2009 to 2.1% of their employment in Japan by 2015.[34] The existing and potential customers can discover and outsource suitable jobs for the Center once they recognize the ultimate purpose of the operations and their unique workforce. There are many individuals who are ignorant about the Center. Once the purpose is clearly understood, there are no concerns, especially about suitable jobs that can be outsourced to the Center.

It is truly hoped the similar commitments as Denso Corporation will be found in the Blount County community to promote opportunities for the TRC Maryville location in the near future.

Noriko through her journey as an MBA student found how her knowledge of operations management could assist others with their problems.

---

[33] Global Denso by Denso Corporation

[34] Global Denso by Denso Corporation

The MBA project was the first, small step to opening the door of undiscovered opportunities. Sometimes it requires courage, time and energy to take that small first step.

Those small steps can be added up to support the operations of other nonprofit organizations. The possibility of people who can benefit from any other nonprofit organizations and who are encouraged by the organizations to take the next step to a more meaningful life is infinite.

We encounter tragedies and human suffering without clear understanding and reasons. It is not meant to hurt us by God's intention but to bring hope and future. Directing attention and energy to something new and more profound reduced Noriko's resistance to cancer. Surviving cancer helped her become more mindful and appreciative of daily activities and the gifts of God. Reaching out to others is part of the healing processes. Given a second chance, Noriko took the steps for positive impact to others who have been through much suffering. The steps were not hard to take because the small car part and the MBA program created the path for her. Life is too short. When we can, let us embrace the opportunities.

"Nobody can go back and start a new beginning, but anyone can start today and make a new ending."

– Maria Robinson

Chapter Notes

INTRODUCTION

Tennessee Department of Human Services, Vocational Rehabilitation Services. (2011). Tennessee Division of Rehabilitation Services State Plan for Fiscal Year 2011 (Draft). http://www.state.tn.us/humanserv/rehab/2011_stateplan.pdf (accessed 2 January 2011).

CHAPTER 1

Davis, Sharon. (2010, November 22). Center Secretary. (N. Chapman, Interviewer).

Hampson, Rick. "In America's next decade, change and challenges." USA Today, (2010). http://www.usatoday.com/news/nation/2010-01-04-2020-the-next-decade_N.htm (accessed 26 April 2010).

Jacobs, Robert, Richard Chase, & Nicholas Aquilano. Operation's & Supply Management. New York: McGraw-Hill Irwin, 2009.

Shim, Jae & Joel Siegel. Operations Management. United State of America: Barren's Educational Series, Inc, 1999.

Closerware.com. "Non-profit market" (2009). http://www.closerware.com/cw/npo.jsp?pg=join1 (accessed 1 January 2011).

McNamara, Carter. "Basic overview of non-profit organizations," (2010). http://managementhelp.org/org_thry/np_thry/np_intro.htm (accessed 1 January 2011).

Tennessee Department of Human Services. (2011). Human Services - About Us. http://www.state.tn.us/humanserv/us.html (accessed 2 January 2011).

Tennessee Department of Human Services, Vocational Rehabilitation Services. (2011).

Tennessee Division of Rehabilitation Services State Plan for Fiscal Year 2011 (Draft). http://www.state.tn.us/humanserv/rehab/2011_stateplan.pdf (accessed 2 January 2011).

CHAPTER 2

Blackbaud.com. "More than 900 nonprofit professionals take steps to improve accountability," (2004). http://www.blackbaud.com/default.aspx?pgpId=2532&PRID=160 (accessed 1 January 2011).

Campaign Consultation. "Understanding trends impacting nonprofit organizations' budgets," (2003). http://www.nationalserviceresources.org/practices/17595 (accessed 1 January 2011).

Closerware.com. "Non-profit market" (2009). http://www.closerware.com/cw/npo.jsp?pg=join1 (accessed 1 January 2011).

CHAPTER 3

Burchfield, Lisa. (2010, November 17). Rehabilitation Technician. (N. Chapman, Interviewer)

Holmes, David. Outcomes Management and Strategic Planning Report. Smyrna: Tennessee Rehabilitation Center, 2009.

Lewis, Allen. (2008). Vocational rehabilitation in the 21st century: Skills professionals need for systems success. Work , 345-356.

Quillen, Deborah. (2010, October 11). Center Manager. (N. Chapman, Interviewer)

CHAPTER 4

Andrew, Jason. The Disability Handbook. Fayetteville: University of Arkansas, 2008.

Brown, Bruce. (2010, October 11). Vocational Educator. (N. Chapman, Interviewer)

Quillen, Deborah. (2010, October 11). Center Manager. (N. Chapman, Interviewer)

CHAPTER 5

Burchfield, Lisa. (2010, November 17). Rehabilitation Technitian. (N. Chapman, Interviewer)

Quillen, Deborah. (2010, October 11). Center Manager. (N. Chapman, Interviewer)

CHAPTER 6

Denso Taiyo Co.,LTD. (n.d.). Company Profile. http://www.aichi-taiyonoie.co.jp/denso_taiyo.html (accessed 29 October 2010).

Holmes, David. Outcomes Management and Strategic Planning Report. Smyrna: Tennessee Rehabilitation Center, 2009.

Quillen, Deborah. (2010, October 11). Center Manager. (N. Chapman, Interviewer)

CONCLUSION

Denso Corporation. (2010). Global Denso. http://www.globaldenso.com/en/esr/employee/workplace.html (accessed 29 October 2010).

Green, Daryl. Breaking Organizational Ties. United States of America: Lulu.com Publisher, 2010.

Kuptsch, Christiane & Eng Fong Pang. Competing for Global Talent. Geneva: International Labour Office and Wee Kim Wee Centre, 2006.

Arizona State University. "Job search strategies in tough economic times." (2010).
http://students.asu.edu/career/strategies_article
(accessed 27 April 2010).

Shalash, Samieh. "Obama to Hampton University graduates: 'be role models for your brothers and sisters'." (10 May 2010).
http://articles.dailypress.com/2010-05-10/news/dp-local_hu-obama-speech_0510may10_1_role-models-graduates-barack-obama
(accessed 10 May 2010).

WTKR. "Transcript of President Barack Obama's commencement address to Hampton University." (10 May 2010).
http://www.wtkr.com/news/wtkr-obama-hampton-address-transcript,0,7478536.story?page=1 (accessed 10 May 2010).

About the Authors

Noriko Chapman is the mother of two children. She lives in Maryville, Tennessee. She is a Production Control supervisor in the Instrument Cluster Division of DENSO Manufacturing Tennessee, Inc. She worked at DENSO specializing in production planning, new products start up, service parts operations, supply chain and warehouse operations for 16 years and for 2 years as a full- or part-time translator at the beginning before the first Tennessee DENSO plant was built. Given the fact that she was raised in Japan, she wrote a chapter "Japanese Practices in an Autoparts Plant" for the book, Effects of Japanese Investment In a Small American Community by Scott Brunger and Young-Bae Kim. Her Maryville College undergraduate research paper, "A Dramaturgical Analysis of Japanese Organization Behavior" won an undergraduate award by North Central Sociological Association. She is currently attending Lincoln Memorial University MBA program and now serves on the board of directors for the Tennessee Department of Human Services, Division of Rehabilitation Services.

If you would like her to speak to your organization or would like more information about her project, please contact:

PMLA
P.O. Box 32733
Knoxville, TN 37930-2733
Phone: (865) 379-6455
Email: Chance2.Noriko@gmail.com

 Dr. Daryl D. Green is a management strategist and a nationally recognized lecturer. He has over 20 years of assisting organizations and individuals with making good decisions. Before his 30th birthday, he had already managed over 400 projects, estimated at $100 million dollars. His professional experience includes management, engineering, research and development, marketing, and personal coaching. He is an adjunct professor at Lincoln Memorial University. He has also been a faculty member at Knoxville College. Currently, Dr. Green is the author of several books and writes a syndicated online column on contemporary issues where over 3,000 online publishers/content providers around the globe have used his articles. He has also been a freelance writer and guest columnist for various publications, including Knoxville News Sentinel, Knoxville Enlightener, Discovery Magazine, and the IEEE Technology and Society Magazine. Additionally, Dr. Green has been noted and quoted by USA Today, Ebony Magazine, and the Associated Press.

He received a B.S. in mechanical engineering and an MA in Organizational Management. Dr. Green received a doctoral degree in strategic leadership from Regent University.

He is a past talk show host, a nationally recognized lecturer, nationally syndicated columnist, and personal advisor.

These experiences place him in a unique position for understanding emerging trends.

If you would like him to speak to your organization or would like more information about his company services, please contact:

PMLA

P.O. Box 32733

Knoxville, TN 37930-2733

Phone: (865) 602-7858

Email: advice@darylgreen.org

Home page: www.darylgreen.org

Other Books by Dr. Green

Dr. Green continues to research and produce information that better society. Below is a synopsis of some of his other products:

A Call to Destiny: How to Create Effective Ways to Assist Black Boys in America provides a practical assessment of what happens to young black boys in America. It seeks to provide ways for parents, educators, and supporters to assist these boys in their positive development. Without any intervention, young black boys, regardless of their social class, will not survive in the 21st century. In this book A Call to Destiny, you will (a) examine the severity of the problems facing young black boys, (b) learn new strategies to bring solutions to your child and the community at large, and (c) provide inspiration to continue the fight to save this generation of boys.
(Paperback: 50 pages, ISBN-13: 978-1442181021)

Awakening the Talents Within is a powerful, step by step approach that individuals can use to solve problems and contribute to their overall success. This book is a wake up call for the next generation of leaders. Green uses his charismatic style for today's hip hop culture, dealing with a wide range of issues from stopping procrastination to creating business ownership. The solutions contained in the book reflect over ten years of managing, consulting, and teaching in government, nonprofit, business, private and academic institutions.
(Paperback: 136 pages, ISBN: 978-0595146130, Hardcover: 140 pages, ISBN: 978-0595745722)

Book Publishing for Professionals provides the secrets of gaining this useful power. Packed with proven insights and advice, this book provides a simple, logical step for professionals. It includes effective writing tools, best publishing options, and marketing strategies to make your book successful in the marketplace. It is geared toward the writer who wants to write a non-fiction book (biography, cookbook, self-help, Christian book, textbook, etc.). (Paperback: 68 pages, ISBN: 978-1449985561, Kindle: 68 ASIN: B0047T7DPA,Hardcover: 108 pages, ISBN: 978-0-557-98346-9, DVD: 26 minutes, ASIN: B001FB4Z3G, CD: 26 minutes, ASIN: B004CYFBBS)

Breaking Organizational Ties provides practical strategies for employees attempting to cope in jobs or environments which they hate. While most managers are only concerned with the bottom-line, they leave their employees vulnerable to the casualties of competitive markets. This book will enable readers to (a) learn how to survive and even enjoy your time at work even in a hostile environment, (b) gain greater confidence in your ability to grow while in a downsizing organization, and (c) discover the insight to go beyond your limitations by breaking the barriers of your self-doubt. (Paperback:124, ISBN: 978-1450511315, Kindle:124, ASIN: B003L77PBQ, Hardcover: 124 pages, ISBN: 978-0557388714)

More Than A Conqueror: Achieving Personal Fulfillment in Government Service is a message about how to take positive steps in achieving your goals while in government service. However, many individuals will be able to benefit from this book. In More than a Conqueror, you will (a) go beyond your self-imposed limitations by breaking the barrier of your self-doubt and (b) protect and cultivate your life in order to bring forth the best you can in your generation. (Paperback: 76 pages, ISBN: 978-0971400887)

My Cup Runneth Over: Setting Goals for Single Parents and Working Couples guides families in setting goals for themselves. Daryl and his wife have first-hand experience on this subject, both working full-time jobs, and raising three active children. This book uses a new management process called Meshing TM. The book is very different from most family books, focusing more on practical solutions. Daryl has used his experience as manager from the government, nonprofit, and private business sectors to assist families in this country to do what we have done--take control of our family. Written in an informal, entertaining style, it provides information to families that give them HOPE. Creatively illustrated with graphics and charts, the book is also indexed for quick reference. It is essential reading for families in search of purpose.

Special Awards: January Book of the Month, The Larry Young Show 1998, Special Black History Award at Atkins Library, Featured on Heaven 600 (The Top Gospel Radio Station in the Country). (Paperback: 108 pages, ISBN: 978-1889745039, Audiobook: 978-1889745053, Audio CD: ASIN: B001VH787E)

Appendices

Appendix A

Discussion Questions

These discussion questions can be used in reading groups or classroom settings.

- What is the priority in your life?

- How do you handle adversity while working or enrolled in school?

- What are the obstacles that could keep you from chasing your dreams?

- How have you been helping others in the community?

- How can organizations become good corporate citizens?

- How can managers make social, economic or environmental contributions to the community?

- How can governments recognize the needs and provide support to nonprofit organizations to operate more effectively and efficiently?

Appendix B

Dedication to Other Cancer Survivors

Noriko is blessed to have her health back and enjoys spending time again with her two sons. The cancer was a life changing experience for her children also. All the support and prayers her family received were transformed positively in the young children's lives. On the day Noriko was diagnosed with cancer, she sat down with her sons and explained the disease to them. She also told them to continue to have fun, get education and dream big. A year after, her 12-year-old son, Zane remembered the conversation and included it in his poem for his school project. This poem is dedicated with prayers to other cancer survivors and their families to find hope in the healing process:

Zane Chapman's Poem:

My Mom - by Zane Chapman (8/5/2010)

My hero is my mom. She is always nice to others. She loves to travel all across the world. She is always very optimistic, even in hard times. In my opinion, she is the best person in the world.

One reason she is nice is because she works very hard to support her family. She goes to work every day and deals with people and does lots of work. She cooks for her family, pays all the bills, and pays for all the groceries. She helps people who are having a hard time. She cares about people; she helps them, she protects them, and she makes them feel better.

Also, my mom is a world traveler. She has been to 28 different countries all around the world. She's been to the U.S., France, Switzerland, Germany, the Bahamas, Jamaica, and many, many more. She always plans entertaining trips inside and outside the U.S. She has planned trips for me to places such as Las Vegas, Denver, Japan, Paris, Jamaica, the Bahamas, Orlando, and Philadelphia. One thing she really loves about traveling is the food. She always has to eat the best food wherever she goes.

Another thing I like about my mom is she is always optimistic no matter what. When she was diagnosed with cancer in 2009, she thought about getting better instead of dying from the disease. She thought about her children's education. She thought about them having fun and playing sports. In late 2009, after her results from surgery, she found out that the cancer was gone and had not spread. So she didn't have to do radiation or chemotherapy.

She always looks on the bright side of every tragedy, recession, or death. Obstacles in life never hold her back from her dreams and goals.

In all, she is the strongest, nicest, and most adventurous person in the world. She tries her best to not be mean to anybody, even if they're mean to her. She doesn't let anything stop her in her tracks. She is always adventurous and upbeat. I admire her because of the reasons.

Appendix C

Tennessee Rehabilitation Centers

Under the Tennessee Department of Human Service, the Tennessee Rehabilitation Center of Blount County is a community resource and employment service assisting businesses in recruiting, hiring, and retaining employees with disabilities. Corporate Connections customizes a full range of employment services including technical assistance and consultation to meet the needs of local companies.

The Tennessee Rehabilitation Center of Blount County provides services that lead to employment and are designed to meet individual needs.

Comprehensive Vocational Evaluation Services

- Determine work interests and abilities
- Career exploration and planning

Employee Development Services

- Perform actual work for area businesses
- Build physical work tolerance
- Learn work skills and gain work experience

Job Development and Employee Assistance

- Job readiness instruction
- Resume development
- Job search assistance

An individual with a disability may apply directly or be referred by an individual or agency. A referral may be made by contacting the Tennessee Rehabilitation Center of Blount County in person, by US postal, or by telephone.

Community Tennessee Rehabilitation Center
1749 Triangle Park Drive
Maryville, Tennessee 37801-3750
(865) 981-2382